Wild Britain

Hedgehog

Louise and Richard Spilsbury

www.heinemann.co.uk
Visit our website to find out more information about **Heinemann Library** books.

To order:
☎ Phone 44 (0) 1865 888066
 Send a fax to 44 (0) 1865 314091
 Visit the Heinemann Bookshop at www.heinemann.co.uk to browse our catalogue and order online.

First published in Great Britain by Heinemann Library, Halley Court, Jordan Hill, Oxford OX2 8EJ, part of Harcourt Education Ltd. Heinemann is a registered trademark of Harcourt Education Ltd.

Editorial: Lucy Thunder and Helen Cox
Design: David Poole and Celia Floyd
Illustrations: Jeff Edwards, Alan Fraser and Geoff Ward
Picture Research: Catherine Bevan and Maria Joannou
Production: Séverine Ribierre

Originated by Dot Gradations
Printed and bound in Hong Kong, China by South China Printing

ISBN 0 431 03931 3
07 06 05 04 03
10 9 8 7 6 5 4 3 2 1

British Library Cataloguing in Publication Data
Spilsbury, Louise and Spilsbury, Richard
Hedgehog. – (Wild Britain)
599.3'32'0941
A full catalogue record for this book is available from the British Library.

Acknowledgements

The Publishers would like to thank the following for permission to reproduce photographs:

Ecoscene p4 (Lillicrap); FLPA pp10, 11 (Derek Middleton), 13, 26 (Tony Hamblin), 19 (B Borrell Casals), 20 (Silvestris Fotoservice), 28 (Eric Woods); ICCE Colour Library p17 (Andy Purcell); Imagestate p14; Natural Science Photos p16 (Tristan Millen); NHPA pp5, 18, 21, 27 (Andy Rouse), 12 (Manfred Danegger), 15 (Roger Tidman), 25 (Daniel Heuclin); Oxford Scientific Films p9; Papilio pp8 (Jamie Harron), 29 (Steve Austin); Premaphotos p24 (Mark Preston-Mafham); RSPCA pp6 (Colin Seddon), 22 (Colin Varndell), 23 (Mark Hamblin).

Cover photograph of a hedgehog, reproduced with permission of The National Trust Photographic Library (Niall Benvine/Nature Picture Library).

The Publishers would like to thank Michael Scott for his assistance in the preparation of this book.

Every effort has been made to contact copyright holders of any material reproduced in this book. Any omissions will be rectified in subsequent printings if notice is given to the Publishers.

Contents

Any words appearing in the text in bold, **like this**, are explained in the Glossary.

What are hedgehogs?

Each spine on a hedgehog's body is 2 to 3 centimetres long. The spines are special hard, prickly hairs.

Hedgehogs are small **mammals** that are covered in **spines**. Adult hedgehogs have about 5000 spines on their sides and back. They have short brown hair on their bellies.

Hedgehogs got their name because they are often seen under hedges and they sometimes squeal like a hog (pig)!

Hedgehogs have short ears, a short tail and a long, pointed nose. An adult is usually about 20 to 30 centimetres long.

Where hedgehogs live

Many hedgehogs live in parks and gardens.

Hedgehogs live where they can find plenty of food and where there are plants to hide among. In Britain, some hedgehogs live in woods, hedges and farmland.

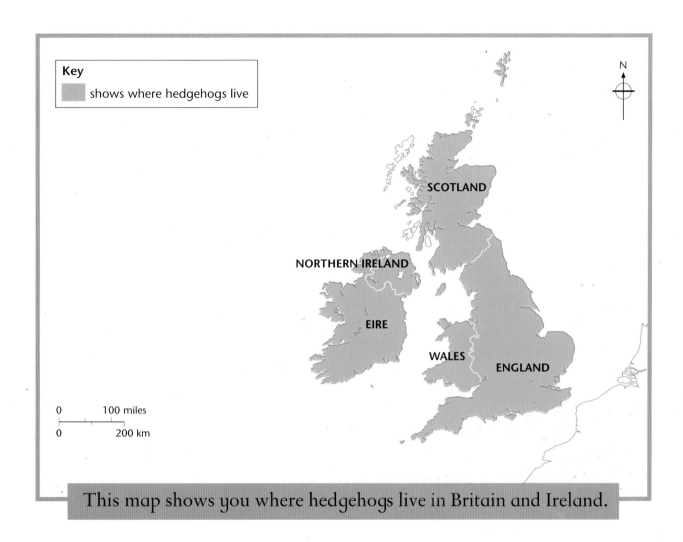

N

SCOTLAND

NORTHERN IRELAND

EIRE

WALES

ENGLAND

0   100 miles

0   200 km

This map shows you where hedgehogs live in Britain and Ireland.

Hedgehogs do not like to live in places where there is nowhere for them to hide. There are no hedgehogs on **moorland** or on wide, open fields without hedges.

What hedgehogs eat

Hedgehogs eat animals that they find or catch on the ground. This hedgehog is eating an earthworm.

Hedgehogs usually feed on **insects**, earthworms, caterpillars, slugs and snails. Sometimes they eat fruit that has fallen to the ground.

Hedgehogs are noisy eaters, especially when crunching snail shells!

Hedgehogs catch food with their mouths. Then they chew it using their 36 small, sharp teeth. They usually make a lot of noise while they eat their food.

Finding food

We do not often see hedgehogs. They only come out to find food at night.

Hedgehogs are **nocturnal**. That means they move around and look for food at night. They are busiest after it has rained – that is when slugs and worms come out.

Hedgehogs often go on the same path each night to find food. They make little tracks on the ground.

Hedgehogs do not see very well. They use their **senses** of smell and hearing to find food in the dark. Many animals that hunt at night find food in this way.

On the move

When a hedgehog runs it holds its legs straight. It also keeps its body off the ground.

Hedgehogs have quite long legs for their body size. They can run quite fast and can climb over low walls. They even swim when they need to!

Hedgehogs have five toes on each foot but their footprints only show four. One toe is small and high up the foot.

Most of the time, hedgehogs shuffle along with their bodies close to the ground. They stop often to sniff the air. They travel up to 2 kilometres a night searching for food.

Resting and sleeping

Hedgehogs rest in quiet places where other animals cannot easily see them.

Hedgehogs rest during the day. They usually sleep in hedges, bramble bushes or among other plants.

This hedgehog is resting among some leaves. It is well hidden.

Hedgehogs rest and sleep in the same place for a few days. Then they move on and find another place to rest in daylight.

Hibernation

Hedgehogs sometimes wake up during hibernation. They find food and water and often build a new nest.

Hedgehogs usually **hibernate** in winter. They sleep in a special **nest** all day and night. Their heartbeat slows down and their bodies go cold to save energy.

Hedgehog nests have a wall of grass and leaves about 10 centimetres thick.

A hedgehog makes a cosy winter nest with leaves and grass. It piles them up in a quiet place. Then it burrows inside and turns round and round to form a cosy nest.

Hedgehog young

The male walks round the female making snuffling noises when it is ready to mate.

Male and **female** hedgehogs **mate** in early summer. Then baby hedgehogs begin to grow inside the female. The babies are born one month later.

Soon after birth, about 100 soft, white spines begin to show on young hedgehogs.

The female gives birth to four or five babies in a **nest** of leaves. A newborn hedgehog is small, blind and has no **spines**. Mother hedgehogs have to feed and care for them.

Growing up

These youngsters are suckling from the mother hedgehog.

Young hedgehogs **suckle** milk from their mother, just like other baby **mammals**. They grow sharp, brown **spines** by eleven days old. Their eyes open at fourteen days old.

Young hedgehogs leave home when they have their adult teeth and can feed themselves.

Young hedgehogs begin to leave the **nest** at three to four weeks old. They still suckle, but can also start to find their own food. At six weeks old they leave to live by themselves.

Hedgehog sounds

When a hedgehog is angry it makes a short coughing sound. It also raises its **spines**.

Hedgehogs are usually silent, but they use sounds to tell each other things. They make lots of different sounds, including puffs, grunts, snorts, coughs and screams.

Hedgehogs make a quiet purring sound when something interests them, like this garden rake!

When a hedgehog is in danger it may squeal like a pig. If another animal comes close, it may puff and sniff sharply. Sleeping hedgehogs often snore!

23

Under attack

Each of these spines is as sharp as a needle. Most animals leave a curled-up hedgehog alone.

A hedgehog curls itself up when it is frightened. It tucks in its head and legs and becomes a ball of spikes. The **spines** hide its soft parts, including its head and tummy.

Foxes are so fast that they catch some hedgehogs before the hedgehogs can curl up.

Badgers and foxes eat hedgehogs. A badger can uncurl a hedgehog with its long claws. Some badgers smell where hedgehogs are **hibernating** and dig them up.

Dangers

Many hedgehogs are killed by cars when they cross roads.

When people cut back hedges they may hurt hedgehogs asleep inside. Some hedgehogs are killed by road traffic. Most hedgehogs only live to two or three years old.

It is important that people do not drop rubbish. Hedgehogs can die if they get stuck inside old jars or tins like this.

Hedgehogs sometimes eat from rubbish that people drop. Broken jars or sharp tins can hurt them. Some people help hedgehogs. They put out pet food or bread and milk for them to eat in winter.

A hedgehog's year

In summer there are more hedgehogs about than in the winter.

Hedgehogs have their young in summer. It is warm then and there are lots of **insects** and slugs for the babies to eat.

Young hedgehogs start hibernation later than adults. This gives them more time to get fat.

Hedgehogs **hibernate** between November and April. They eat as much as they can from May to October. They need to store enough fat to live on when hibernating.

Animal groups

Scientists group together animals that are alike. Hedgehogs are in the same group as shrews and moles. They are all **mammals** with sharp teeth for catching insects.

hedgehog

shrew

mole

The artwork on this page is not to scale.

Glossary

female   animal which can become a mother when it is grown up. A female human is called a woman or a girl.

hibernate   go into a very deep sleep for a long time with little or no food

insect   small animal that has six legs when an adult, such as beetles or flies

male   animal which can become a father when it is grown up. A male human is called a man or a boy.

mammals   group of animals that includes humans. All mammals feed their babies their own milk and have some hair on their bodies.

mate   what a male and female animal do to start a baby growing inside the female

moorland   cool windy area up a hill covered by grasses and heather

nest   shelter an animal makes to rest in or to have young in

nocturnal   active at night and resting during the day

scientist   person who studies the world around us and the things in it to find out how they work

senses   most animals have five senses – sight, hearing, touch, taste and smell

spines   sharp spikes that grow from an animal's back

suckle   when a mother feeds her baby with milk from her body

Index

Titles in the *Wild Britain* series include:

Hardback   0 431 03928 3

Hardback   0 431 03932 1

Hardback   0 431 03930 5

Hardback   0 431 03931 3

Hardback   0 431 03933 X

Hardback   0 431 03929 1

Find out about the other titles in this series on our website www.heinemann.co.uk/library